EXPLORING THE STATES

Utah

THE BEEHIVE STATE

by Blake Hoena

BELLWETHER MEDIA • MINNEAPOLIS, MN

Note to Librarians, Teachers, and Parents:

Blastoff! Readers are carefully developed by literacy experts and combine standards-based content with developmentally appropriate text.

Level 1 provides the most support through repetition of high-frequency words, light text, predictable sentence patterns, and strong visual support.

Level 2 offers early readers a bit more challenge through varied simple sentences, increased text load, and less repetition of high-frequency words.

Level 3 advances early-fluent readers toward fluency through increased text and concept load, less reliance on visuals, longer sentences, and more literary language.

Level 4 builds reading stamina by providing more text per page, increased use of punctuation, greater variation in sentence patterns, and increasingly challenging vocabulary.

Level 5 encourages children to move from "learning to read" to "reading to learn" by providing even more text, varied writing styles, and less familiar topics.

Whichever book is right for your reader, Blastoff! Readers are the perfect books to build confidence and encourage a love of reading that will last a lifetime!

This edition first published in 2014 by Bellwether Media, Inc.

No part of this publication may be reproduced in whole or in part without written permission of the publisher. For information regarding permission, write to Bellwether Media, Inc., Attention: Permissions Department, 5357 Penn Avenue South, Minneapolis, MN 55419.

Library of Congress Cataloging-in-Publication Data

Hoena, B. A.
 Utah / by Blake Hoena.
  pages cm. – (Blastoff! readers. Exploring the states)
 Includes bibliographical references and index.
 Summary: "Developed by literacy experts for students in grades three through seven, this book introduces young readers to the geography and culture of Utah"–Provided by publisher.
 ISBN 978-1-62617-044-5 (hardcover)
 1. Utah–Juvenile literature. I. Title.
 F826.3.H64 2014
 979.2–dc23
                                                                    2013009627

Printed in the United States of America, North Mankato, MN.

Table of Contents

Where Is Utah?

Utah is located in the western United States. It is shaped like a rectangle with the northeastern corner cut out. In that notch sits Wyoming. Idaho forms the rest of Utah's northern border. Nevada lies to the west. Arizona runs along the state's southern edge. Utah shares its eastern border with Colorado. Salt Lake City is Utah's capital and largest city. It is located in the north near Great Salt Lake.

Utah has many stunning rock formations. Towering peaks fill the horizon, and deserts stretch out across the state. Beautiful, rugged land sits inside Utah's straight borders.

Nevada

Pacific Ocean

Idaho

Great Salt Lake

Wyoming

Salt Lake City

West Valley City

Park City

West Jordan

Provo

Utah

Bryce Canyon National Park

Colorado

Arizona

New Mexico

Native Americans lived in Utah when European explorers arrived in the 1700s. In 1847, Brigham Young led the first group of white settlers to Utah. They were seeking a peaceful land to practice their Mormon religion. The United States took control of the area after the Mexican-American War. Utah became the forty-fifth state in 1896.

Brigham Young

Utah Timeline!

1765: Juan María de Rivera is the first European to explore the Utah region.

1847: Brigham Young leads Mormon settlers from Illinois to Utah.

1848: The United States gains control of Utah as a result of the Mexican-American War.

1848: Swarms of grasshoppers invade north-central Utah. Crops are saved when seagulls from Great Salt Lake feast on the insects.

1869: The Union Pacific and Central Pacific Railroads meet at Promontory Summit. This allows for easy travel across the country.

1896: Utah becomes the forty-fifth state.

1928: Bryce Canyon becomes a national park.

2002: Utah hosts the Winter Olympics in Salt Lake City.

Mormon settlers

Promontory Summit

2002 Winter Olympics

The Land

Utah can be divided into three distinct land areas. The Basin and Range Region covers much of the western half of the state. It is a hot, dry area with small mountain ranges, wide valleys, and **barren** deserts. Utah's Great Salt Lake is located there.

The Rocky Mountains run through the northeast. This area is the snowiest and coldest part of the state. Several mountain peaks rise above 13,000 feet (3,962 meters). The Colorado **Plateau** spreads over the southern half of the state. Some of Utah's most stunning **canyons** and plateaus are found in this region.

fun fact

Great Salt Lake earned its name because its water is saltier than ocean water. It is also the largest natural lake in the Western United States.

Great Salt Lake

Zion National Park

Bryce Canyon

Bryce Canyon is one of Utah's most striking national parks. Over millions of years, **erosion** from water and ice sculpted its red rock into stunning forms. The area became a national park in 1928. It was named after **pioneer** Ebenezer Bryce.

Bryce Canyon's best views feature the vast U-shaped
sections of canyon. These **amphitheaters** span the
horizon. Thin, rocky **spires** called *hoodoos* line the
canyon walls. Another amazing sight is Natural Bridge.
It is just one of the many red rock arches in the canyon.

Wildlife

In Utah's drier areas, cactuses, mesquite, and sagebrush are common. The grassy **plains** are speckled with wildflowers. Sego lilies, Indian paintbrushes, and spurred lupines bloom in the warm months. Aspen, fir, and spruce trees flourish in Utah's mountain regions.

Large animals such as black bears and mountain lions roam the mountains. Elks, pronghorns, and mule deer graze in high meadows. Small animals like weasels and beavers are also found in the state. Scorpions, lizards, and snakes scurry about in Utah's desert areas.

Indian paintbrush

mule deer

black bear

California
gulls

**Rainbow Bridge
National Monument**

Utah has many amazing natural landmarks. The Rainbow Bridge National Monument is the largest natural stone bridge in the world. It stands 290 feet (88 meters) tall and 275 feet (84 meters) across in Glen Canyon National Recreation Area. Southern Utah shares Monument Valley with Arizona. The valley boasts sandstone **buttes** that rise 1,000 feet (305 meters).

The two sections of the **Transcontinental** Railroad were connected at Promontory Summit on May 10, 1869. For the first time, people in the east could quickly travel to the western states. The Golden Spike National Historic Site celebrates this event by sharing stories about the railroad's construction.

Golden Spike National Historic Site

Monument Valley

Park City

fun fact

In January, Park City welcomes filmakers from around the world for the Sundance Film Festival. Dozens of independent films hit the big screen at this event.

Park City is located in northern Utah near Salt Lake City. It began as a mining town in 1869. **Prospectors** flooded the area in search of silver. Soon they were building homes and schools for their families. For decades, mining companies found great success and fortune in Park City.

In the late 1900s, Park City became a major **resort** town. The Wasatch Mountains tower over the city and provide year-round fun for outdoor adventurers. Their snowy slopes hosted some of the world's greatest athletes during the 2002 Winter Olympics. Park City is also a proud supporter of the arts. Music and film festivals bring world-famous talent to the lively city every year.

Most of Utah's workers have **service jobs**. Many serve the state's **tourists** at hotels, restaurants, ski resorts, and parks. They also lead fishing, hunting, and canoe trips. Others work for the government.

Mining and **manufacturing** are also important in Utah. The state has rich deposits of oil, natural gas, and coal. Salt mines are located in much of the Basin and Range Region. Gold, silver, and copper are also mined. The state's factory workers make electronics and transportation equipment.

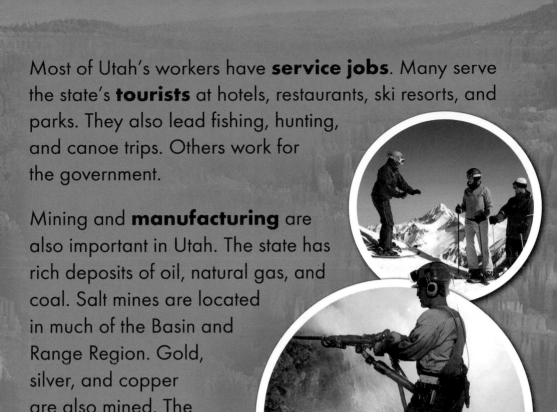

Where People Work in Utah

government
14%

services
76%

farming and
natural resources
2%

manufacturing
8%

Playing

Most Utahans live in cities and towns. They enjoy visiting museums and watching films. They also like to get outdoors. People hike, bike, and ride horses. Mountain lakes and streams are excellent spots for trout fishing. Hunters target mule deer and elks. They also hunt pheasants, wild turkeys, and other **game** birds.

Music has always been important to the people of Utah. Brigham Young brought a brass band with him when he first came to the state. The Mormon Tabernacle Choir was formed in 1847. This famous group of singers entertains audiences around the world.

fun fact !

Utah has one professional sports team, the Utah Jazz. This basketball team has played its home games in Salt Lake City since 1979.

Food

Dutch oven

The Dutch oven is Utah's state cooking pot. Settlers brought these big **cast iron** pots with them when they moved west. Dutch ovens have influenced the food of Utah. People use them to prepare casseroles, stews, breads, and desserts.

One unique Utah food is fry sauce. It is a mix of ketchup, mayonnaise, pickle relish, and spices. Most restaurants serve it as a dipping sauce for french fries. Funeral potatoes are a **traditional** side dish in Utah. This cheesy potato casserole got its name because it was once served at after-funeral dinners. Now it is dished out at most large meals and gatherings.

Fry Sauce

Ingredients:

1 cup mayonnaise

1/2 cup ketchup

1 tablespoon pickle juice

1/2 teaspoon onion powder

Directions:

1. Mix all ingredients together in a small bowl.

2. Refrigerate until use.

3. Serve as a dipping sauce with french fries.

Festivals

The Days of '47 is an event that celebrates Utah's early pioneer days. This festival has something for everyone to enjoy. It features parades, **rodeos**, and dances. Visitors can also experience what life was like when pioneers first arrived in the state.

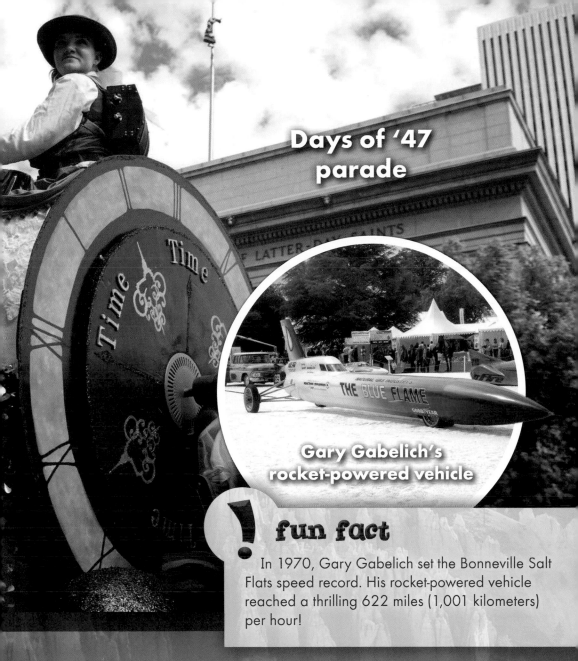

Days of '47 parade

Gary Gabelich's rocket-powered vehicle

! fun fact

In 1970, Gary Gabelich set the Bonneville Salt Flats speed record. His rocket-powered vehicle reached a thrilling 622 miles (1,001 kilometers) per hour!

The Great Salt Lake Desert has open stretches of hard-packed salt. World of Speed is held at the Bonneville Salt Flats. Racers rocket across the flats to see how fast they can go. Hundreds of artists participate in the Utah Arts Festival. This four-day event draws thousands to Salt Lake City.

The Mormon Church

In 1844, Brigham Young became the new leader of the Mormon Church. He led followers from Illinois to the Great Salt Lake Valley in Utah. They were searching for a place to freely practice their religion. Thousands of Mormons later settled in the area.

Mormons belong to the The Church of Jesus Christ of Latter-Day Saints. Today, they make up more than half of Utah's population. Family and community are very important to members of the Mormon Church. Mormons also believe in hard work. These same values helped Utah grow into the beautiful, thriving state it is today.

Brigham
Young

Salt Lake
Tabernacle

Salt Lake
Temple

27

Fast Facts About Utah

Utah's Flag

Utah's flag is blue. In its center is the state seal. It features an eagle hovering over the state motto. In the middle of the seal is a beehive, a symbol of hard work. Around the hive are sego lilies. American flags stream down on either side. Two dates complete the seal. 1847 is the year Mormons first settled in Utah. 1896 is the year Utah became a state.

State Animal
Rocky Mountain elk

State Nicknames:	The Beehive State The Deseret State The Mormon State
State Motto:	"Industry"
Year of Statehood:	1896
Capital City:	Salt Lake City
Other Major Cities:	West Valley City, Provo, West Jordan
Population:	2,763,885 (2010)
Area:	84,897 square miles (219,882 square kilometers); Utah is the 13th largest state.
Major Industries:	services, mining, manufacturing
Natural Resources:	oil, natural gas, gold, silver, copper
State Government:	75 representatives; 29 senators
Federal Government:	4 representatives; 2 senators
Electoral Votes:	6

State Bird
California gull

State Flower
sego lily

Glossary

amphitheaters—large open circles that slope down toward the center

barren—unable to support growth

buttes—small hills or mountains with steep sides and flat tops

canyons—narrow river valleys with steep, tall sides

cast iron—a type of metal that is molded into a desired shape; cast iron pots are very durable and can withstand high temperatures.

erosion—the slow wearing away of soil by water or wind

game—wild animals that are hunted for food or sport

manufacturing—a field of work in which people use machines to make products

native—originally from a specific place

pioneer—one of the first people to explore or settle an area

plains—large areas of flat land

plateau—an area of flat, raised land

prospectors—people who explore an area for natural resources such as oil, silver, or gold

resort—a vacation spot that offers recreation, entertainment, and relaxation

rodeos—events where people compete at tasks such as bull riding and calf roping; cowboys once completed these tasks as part of their daily work.

service jobs—jobs that perform tasks for people or businesses

spires—rock formations that come to a point at the top

tourists—people who travel to visit another place

traditional—relating to a custom, idea, or belief handed down from one generation to the next

transcontinental—extending across a continent

To Learn More

AT THE LIBRARY

Graf, Mike. *Bryce and Zion: Danger in the Narrows.* Golden, Colo.: Fulcrum Pub., 2006.

Sanford, William R. *Brigham Young: Courageous Mormon Leader.* Berkeley Heights, N.J.: Enslow Publishers, 2013.

Tieck, Sarah. *Utah.* Minneapolis, Minn.: ABDO Pub. Co., 2013.

ON THE WEB

Learning more about Utah is as easy as 1, 2, 3.

1. Go to www.factsurfer.com.

2. Enter "Utah" into the search box.

3. Click the "Surf" button and you will see a list of related Web sites.

With factsurfer.com, finding more information is just a click away.

Index

The images in this book are reproduced through the courtesy of: Colin D. Young, front cover (bottom); Charles William Carter/ Harvard Art Museum/ Wikipedia, p. 6; CDGentry/ Wikipedia, p. 7 (left); Everett Collection/ SuperStock, p. 7 (middle); Spirit of America, p. 7 (right); Eric Broder Van Dyke, p. 8 (small); Peter Kunasz, pp. 8-9; Curtis, pp. 10-11; Aron Hsaio, pp. 12-13; Ttphoto, p. 12 (top); Tom Reichner, p. 12 (middle); Wyatt Rivard, p. 12 (bottom); George H.H. Huey/ Age Fotostock/ SuperStock, pp. 14-15; Jerry Susoeff, p. 15 (left); Bryan Busovicki, p. 15 (right); Don Despain/ Alamy, pp. 16-17; Rob Crandall/ Alamy, p. 16 (small); imagebroker.net/ SuperStock, p. 18; Doug Berry Images, p. 19 (top); Craig Aurness/ CORBIS/ GlowImages, p. 19 (bottom); Mike Schirf/ Aurora Open/ SuperStock, pp. 20-21; Ray Stubblebine/ Icon SMI 771/ NewsCom, p. 20 (small); Lincoln Rogers, p. 22; Nilsz, p. 22 (small); Viktor1, p. 23 (left); Africa Studio, p. 23 (right); ZUMA Press, Inc./ Alamy, pp. 24-25; Troxx/ Wikipedia, p. 25 (small); photo.ua, pp. 26-27; H-D Falkenstein/ imagebroker.net/ SuperStock, p. 26 (left); Minyun Zhou, p. 26 (right); Pakmor, p. 28 (top); Tom Reichner, p. 28 (bottom); Ken Hoehn Photography, p. 29 (left); LeavXC/ Wikipedia, p. 29 (right).